THE Beatles
WORDS WITHOUT MUSIC

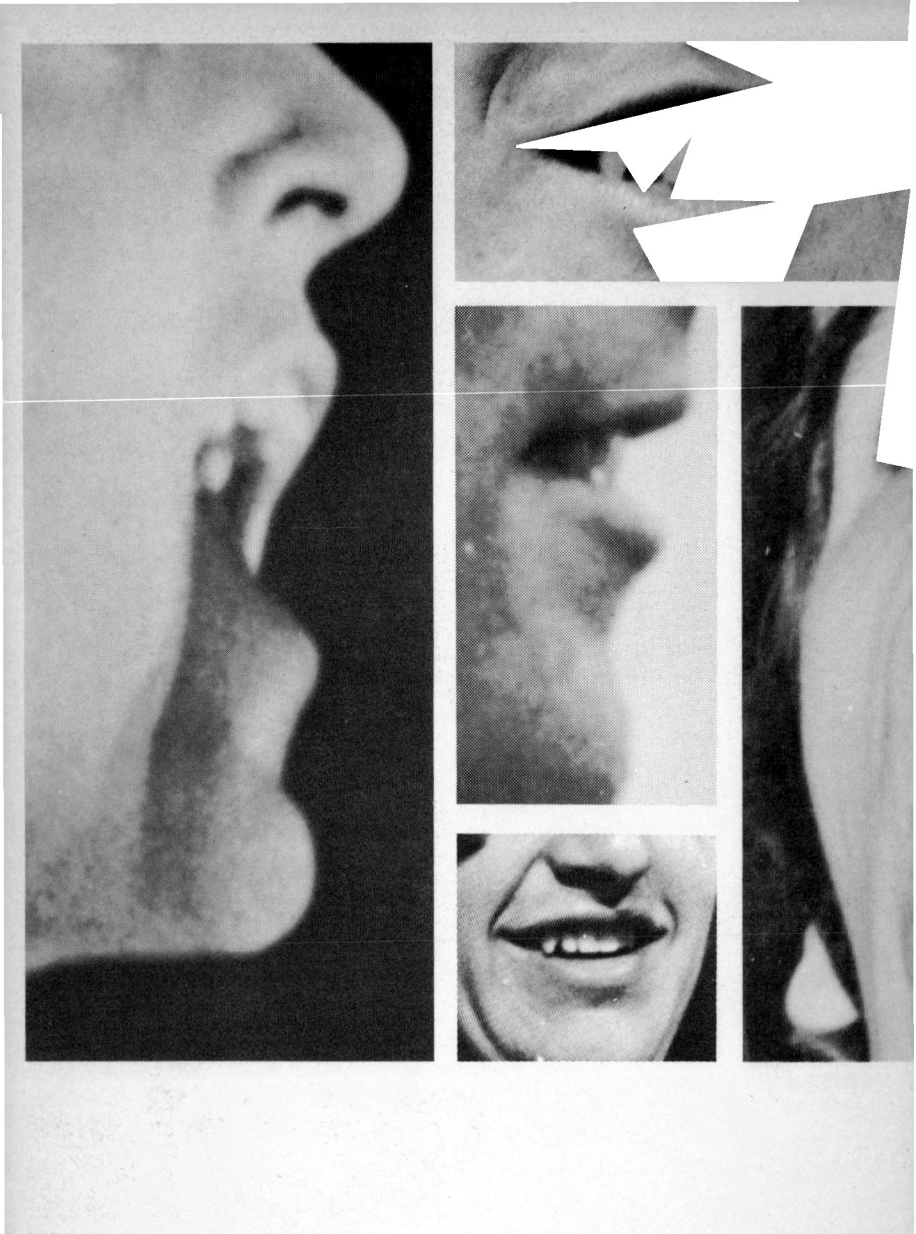

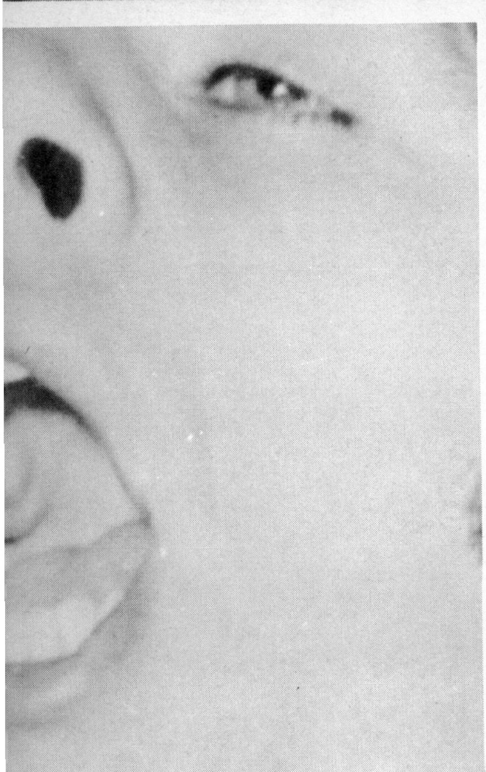

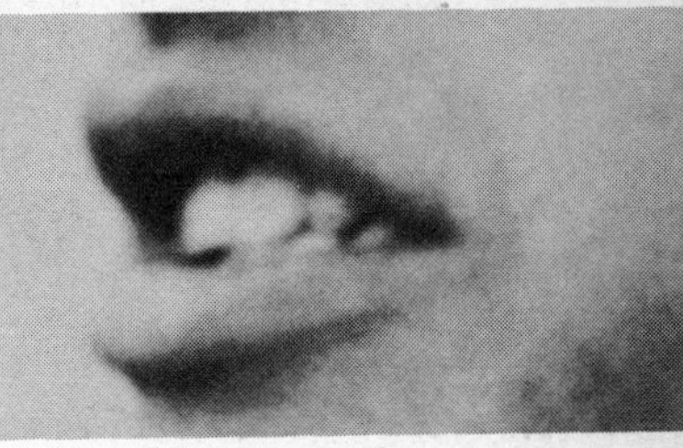

THE Beatles

WORDS WITHOUT MUSIC

Compiled by Rick Friedman
Introduced by Joe O'Brien, wmca radio

WORKMAN PUBLISHING COMPANY, Inc.
Publisher GROSSET & DUNLAP, INC. New York

GROSSET & DUNLAP SPECIAL EDITION 1968
BY ARRANGEMENT WITH WORKMAN PUBLISHING COMPANY, INC.

Library of Congress Catalog Card Number: 68-12742

Published simultaneously in Canada

Cover by Howard Winters
Book designed by Marvin Nudelman

Printed in the United States of America

introduction by **Joe O'Brien** (WMCA Radio)

So many millions of words have been written about the Beatles, that even someone who was there at the beginning and has followed them day in and day out ever since feels overwhelmed when he has to write about them.

It seems ages, but it's been such a short time really, since that day they first arrived in New York and I met them and talked to them and was impressed. Impressed is the wrong word. Bowled over would be more accurate. And so was pop music for all time.

It took about two years before the American press finally realized the importance of the Beatles—not just their wealth and fame—and only recently this same press has gone to

great lengths to explain them to us. But in my opinion, this book explains John, Paul, George and Ringo much more dynamically and accurately than all the endless articles in the endless magazines and newspapers. Never mind what the hack magazine writers or the slick magazine writers or the suburb-based TV pundits or the academicians or the psychiatrists say, the book contains what the Beatles say—about themselves. Now, a person's opinion of himself is very often unrevealing and invalid; at times downright nonsense. But the circumstances under which the Beatles answered every conceivable question hurled at them forced them to give immediate and spontaneous responses. And I think you will find, as I did, that these answers are very revealing. First of all, I'd forgotten how genuinely funny they are. And I mean all four. I remember when they first arrived in New York. It was fashionable then to say that the Beatles were putting the whole world on. And they were to a certain extent. But as I read the manuscript of this book you are about to read, I was amazed at the sheer wit and humor that all four were capable of in completely ad-lib situations.

But what really makes the book fascinating is how the answers pinpoint the differences in their outlooks, interests, etc. and also the similarities. For example, you will find as you read the book that all four are capable of the silly put-down answer, not just John and Ringo. Pick out your favorites and ask yourself whatever became of the person who asked the question. Now, the differences can make a great game. You play it like this: someone reads a question and an answer and the contestants guess whose answer it is. You'll find after a couple of rounds that you are becoming better and better at it because the answers reveal the identities more completely than anything I've ever read.

But read the book. I know you'll laugh and enjoy it, and you'll appreciate the great selection of pictures too. If you are a confirmed Beatle aficionado, you'll say "At last!". If you're not, you will be when you finish reading. As Paul said when a reporter asked him if the Beatles' popularity was tapering off: "I agree that our popularity has hit a peak. But I also agreed with a man who said that same thing last year. And we were both wrong."

hello goodbye

Q: How did you find America?
RINGO: We went to Greenland and made a left turn.

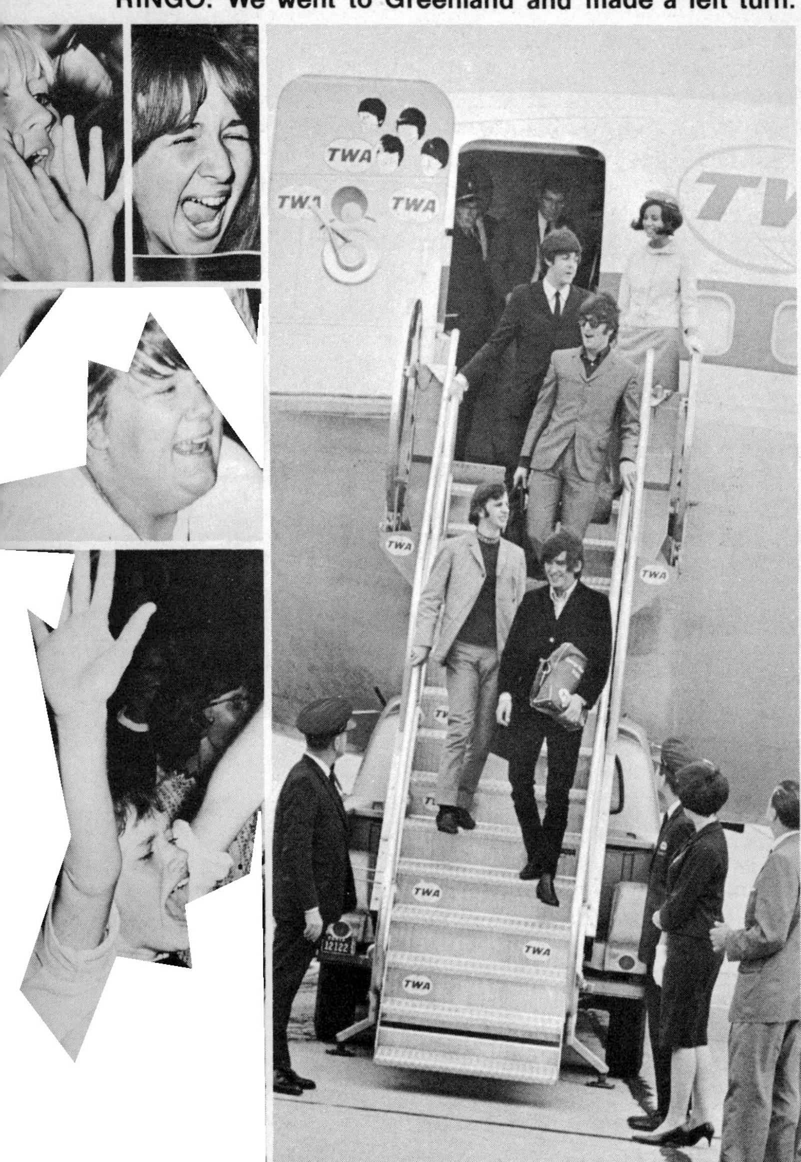

Q: What started your practice of wearing four rings at once?
RINGO: Six got to be too heavy.

Q: Why do you think you get more fan mail than anyone else in the group?
RINGO: I dunno. Suppose it's because more people write me.

Q: Do you date much?
RINGO: What are you doing tonight?

Q: How tall are you?
RINGO: Two feet, nine inches.

Q: Do you like fish and chips?
RINGO: Yes. But I like steak and chips better.

Q: Do you like topless bathing suits?
RINGO: We've been wearing them for years.

Q: Why don't you like Donald Duck?
RINGO: I could never understand him.

Q: Do you resent fans ripping up your sheets for souvenirs?
RINGO: No, I don't mind. So long as I'm not in them while the ripping is going on.

Q: What did you think of Miami?
RINGO: The sun. I didn't know what it meant until I got there. But I am breathtaken to be back in England.

Q: Were you worried about the over-sized roughnecks who tried to infiltrate the airport crowd on your arrival?
RINGO: That was us.

Q: How does it feel puttin
on the whole world?
RINGO: We enjoy it.
PAUL: We aren't really put-ting you on.
GEORGE: Just a bit of it.
JOHN: How does it feel t be put on?

ringo in my life

Q: Does all the adulation from teenage girls affect you?
JOHN: When I feel my head start to swell, I look at Ringo and know perfectly well we're not supermen.

Q: How do you write your books?
JOHN: I put things down on sheets of paper and stuff them in my pockets. When I have enough, I have a book.

Q: What's the most unusual request you've had?
JOHN: I wouldn't like to say.

Q: What excuse do you have for your collar-length hair?
JOHN: Well, it just grows out y'er head.

Q: Girls rushed toward my car because it had press identification and they thought I met you. How do you explain this phenomenon?
JOHN: You're lovely to look at.

Q: How do you stand in the draft?
JOHN: About 5 feet, 11 inches.

Q: What about your future?
JOHN: It looks nice.

Q: Would you like to walk down the street without being recognized?
JOHN: We used to do this with no money in our pockets. There's no point in it.

Q: Are you scared when crowds scream at you?
JOHN: More so in Dallas than in other places, perhaps.

Q: Where would you like to go if all the security wasn't necessary?
JOHN: Harlem.

john in my life

Q: How do you feel about other Beatle-type groups?
JOHN: The Rolling Stones are personal friends of ours. They are most creative and beginning to write good songs.

Q: Do you like being Beatles?
JOHN: Yes, or we'd be the Rolling Stones.

Q: Do you plan to record any anti-war songs?
JOHN: All our songs are anti-war.

Q: Is it true you can't sing?
JOHN: (pointing to George) **Not me. Him.**

Q: When are you starting your next movie?
PAUL: In February
GEORGE: We have no title for it yet.
RINGO: We have no story for it yet.
JOHN: We have no actors for it yet.

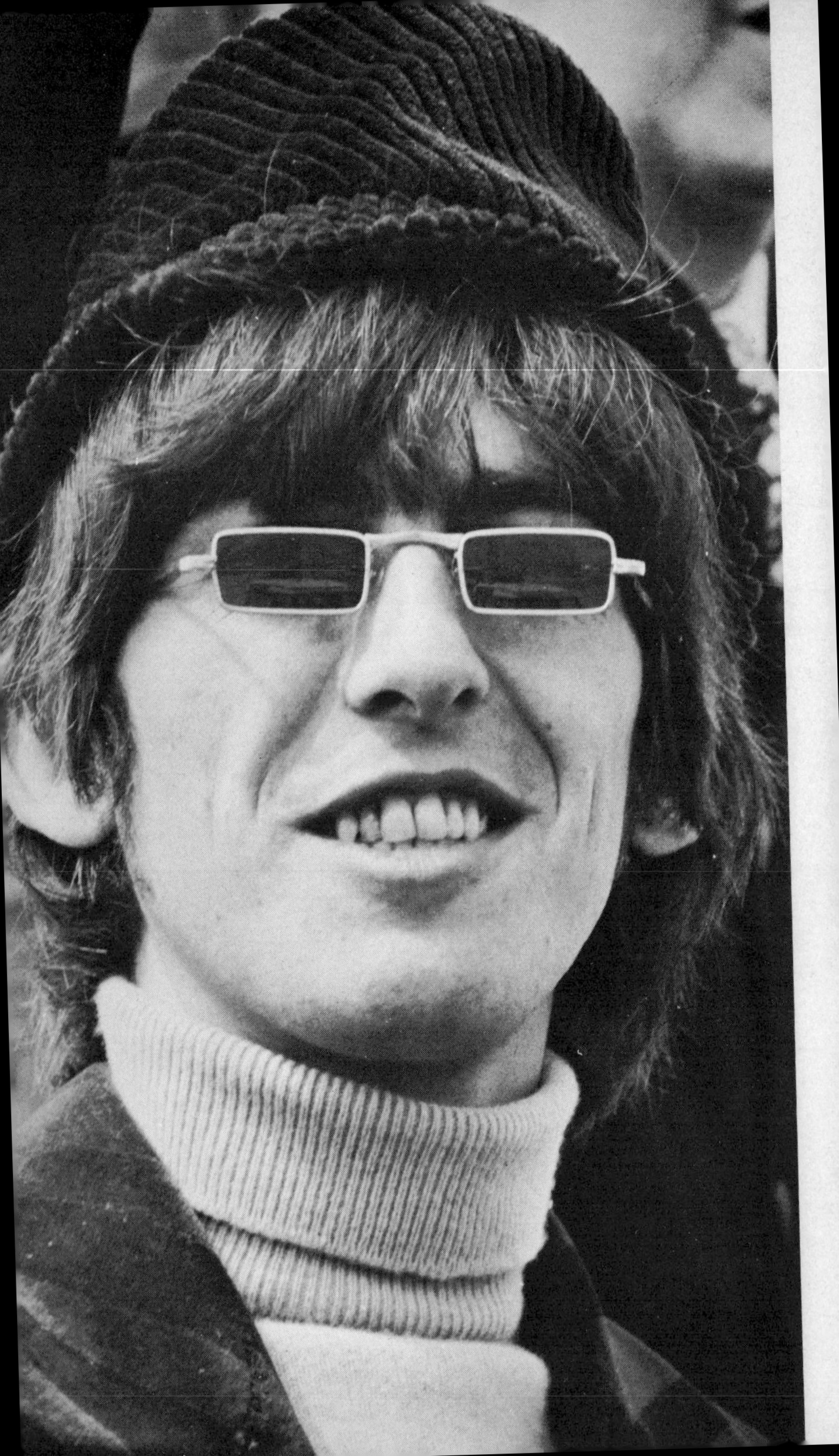

george in my life

Q: Why don't you smile, George?
GEORGE: I'll hurt my lips.

Q: What is your reaction to a Seattle psychiatrist's opinion that you are a menace?
GEORGE: Psychiatrists are a menace.

Q: What's this about an annual illness, George?
GEORGE: I get cancer every year.

Q: How do you feel about a night club, Arthur, named after your hair style?
GEORGE: I was proud—until I saw the night club.

Q: What do you consider the most important thing in life?
GEORGE: Love.

Q: What is *your* personal goal?
GEORGE: To do as well as I can at whatever I attempt. And someday to die with a peaceful mind.

Q: But you really don't expect that to happen for a long time yet, do you?
GEORGE: When your number's oop, it's oop.

"The Beatles' strong beat seems to awaken echoes of significant early experiences such as the fetal intrauterine serenity that repetitively reverberates to the mother's heartbeat."

—Ner Littner,
Chicago Psychiatrist

Q: Why do teenagers stand up and scream piercingly and painfully when you appear?
PAUL: None of us know. But we've heard that teenagers go to our shows just to scream. A lot of them don't even want to listen because they have our records.

Q: Do you like making movies?
PAUL: It's not a bad way to get through an afternoon.

Q: Do you plan to marry Jane Asher?
PAUL: I've got no plans. But everybody keeps saying I have. Maybe they know better. They say I'm married and divorced, and have fifty kids. So you might as well, too.

Q: What kind of music do you like?
PAUL: Colored American groups.

Q: What is your reaction to composers Aaron Copland, who found the Beatles' music interesting, and Richard Rodgers, who found it boring?
PAUL: I like anyone who says he likes our music. I don't mind Richard Rodgers saying he finds it boring—but I must add that I find Richard Rodgers' music boring. And I'm not being nasty, Richard.

Q: Who thought up the name, Beatles?
PAUL: I thought of it.
Q: Why?
PAUL: Why not?

Q: There's a "Stamp Out the Beatles" movement under way in Detroit. What are you going to do about it?
PAUL: We're going to start a campaign to stamp out Detroit.

paul in my life

Q: Do you fight amongst yourselves?
JOHN: Only in the mornings.

Q: What do you miss most now that your fame prohibits your freedom?
RINGO: Going to the movies.
GEORGE: Having nothing to do.
JOHN: School, because you don't have much to do there.
PAUL: Going on buses.

Q: What impresses you most about America?
JOHN: Bread.
PAUL: Going on buses.

Q: Why are your speaking voices different from your singing voices?
GEORGE: We don't have a musical background.

Q: When you do a new song, how do you decide who sings the lead?
JOHN: We just get together and whoever knows most of the words sings the lead.

Q: How do you keep your psychic balance?
RINGO: The important thing is not to get potty. There's four of us, so whenever one of us gets a little potty, the other three bring him back to earth.

Q: What do you do when you're cooped up in a hotel room between shows?
GEORGE: We ice skate.

Q: Paul, what do you think of columnist Walter Winchell?
PAUL: He said I'm married and I'm not.
GEORGE: Maybe he wants to marry you.

(Twelve thousand screaming fans converge on London Airport to welcome the Beatles home.)

"I warned them not to land on a weekend! The next time the Beatles come in or go out of this airport, it will *have* to be on a school day!"

—*F.L. Passmore, airport manager*

sgt. pepper's lonely hearts club band

"They're up in the room playing Monopoly and cards. They are virtual prisoners everywhere they go. It's a pretty horrible life...it's lucky they are so fond of each other."
—A General Artist Corporation booking agent

run for your life

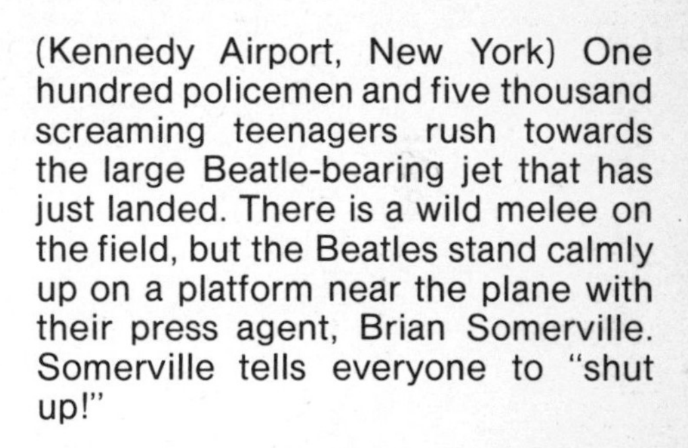

(Kennedy Airport, New York) One hundred policemen and five thousand screaming teenagers rush towards the large Beatle-bearing jet that has just landed. There is a wild melee on the field, but the Beatles stand calmly up on a platform near the plane with their press agent, Brian Somerville. Somerville tells everyone to "shut up!"

The Beatles are carried high in the air through the screeching crowd by policemen and placed in separate Cadillac limousines.

•

(Miami International Airport, Florida) Four thousand hysterical teenagers batter down doors, smash windows and swarm through police lines to greet the Beatles. Thirty students suffer cuts on the arms and face when they surge through an arm-to-arm police blockade and break two glass doors.

Q: How do you like this welcome?
RINGO: So this is America. They all seem out of their minds.

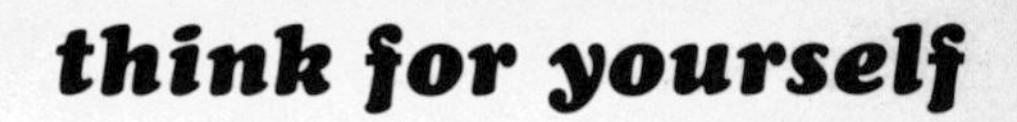

think for yourself

Q: Beethoven figures in one of your songs. What do you think of Beethoven?
RINGO: He's great. Especially his poetry.

Q: Do you believe in lunacy?
RINGO: Yeah. It's healthy.

Q: But aren't you embarrassed by all the lunacy?
RINGO: No. It's crazy.

Q: Ringo, why do you wear two rings on each hand?
RINGO: Because I can't fit them through my nose.

Q: What do you think of Christine Keeler?
RINGO: She's a great comic.

Q: Do you think it's wrong to set such a bad example to teenagers, smoking the way you do?
RINGO: It's better than being alcoholics.

Q: What do you think of the criticism you are not very good?
GEORGE: We're not.

Q: What do you believe is the reason you are the most popular singing group today?
JOHN: We've no idea. If we did, we'd get four long-haired boys, put them together and become their managers.

Q: You've admitted to being agnostics. Are you also irreverent?
PAUL: We are agnostics, so there is no point in being irreverent.

Q: Why are you disinterested in politics?
JOHN: We're not. We just think politicians are disinteresting.

Q: What do you think of the Vietnam war?
JOHN: We think of it every day. We don't like it. We don't agree with it. We think it is wrong. But there is not much we can do about it. All we can do is say we don't like it.

Q: What is your opinion of Americans who go to Canada to avoid the draft?
JOHN: We're not allowed opinions.
PAUL: Anybody who feels that fighting is wrong has the right not to go in the army.
JOHN: We all just don't agree with war. There's no need for anyone to kill for any reason.
GEORGE: Thou shalt not kill means that—not "Amend Section A." There's no reason whatsoever. No one can force you to kill anyone if you don't want to.

Q: What do you think you've contributed to the musical field?
RINGO: Records.
GEORGE: A laugh and a smile.

Q: Do you care what the public thinks about your private lives?
RINGO: There's a woman in the United States who predicted the plane we were travelling on would crash. Now a lot of people would like to think we were scared into saying a prayer. What we did actually—we drank.

Q: What do you think of space shots?
JOHN: You see one, you've seen them all.

Q: What do you think about the pamphlet calling you four Communists?
PAUL: Us, Communists? Why we can't be Communists. We're the world's number one Capitalists. Imagine us Communists!

Q: What about the recent criticism of your lyrics?
PAUL: If you start reading things into them, you might just as well start singing hymns.

"The Beatles are a plot by the British ruling classes to distract British youngsters from politics and bitter pondering over disgraced and shattered hopes."

— *Komsomolskava Pravda*

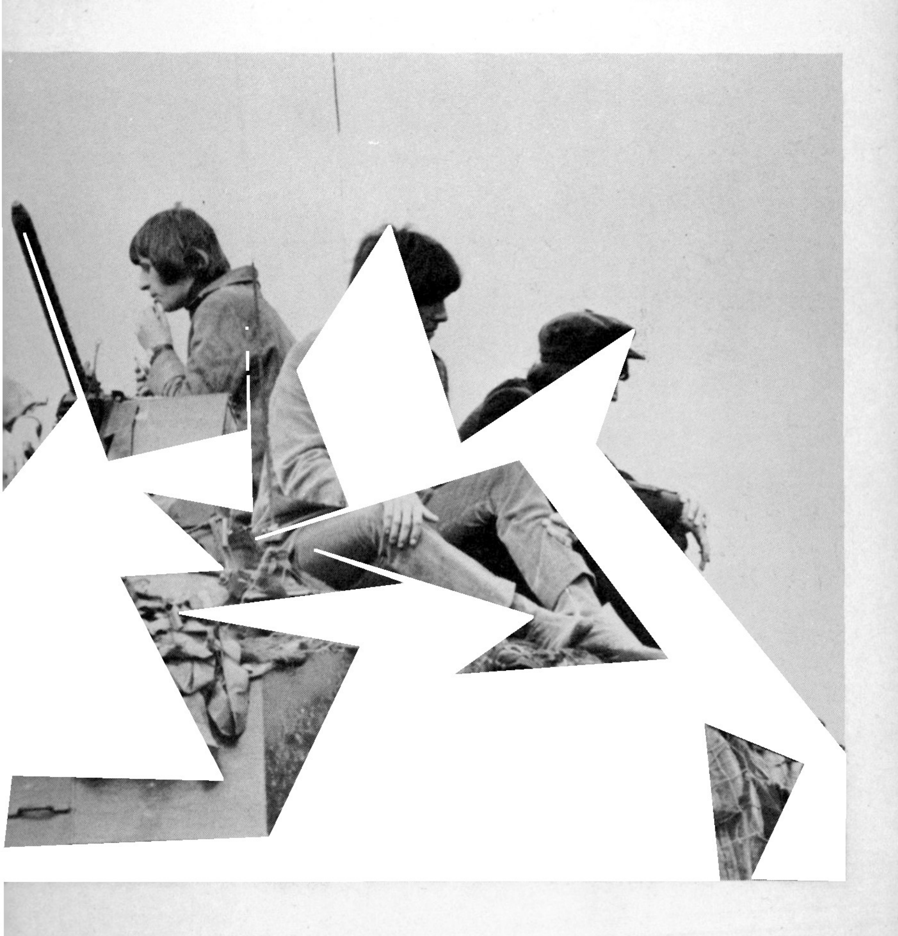

penny lane

"They are the only performers in the history of show business who have made a million dollars for letting the audience entertain them."

James Bacon, AP movie writer

Q: Beatle-licensed products have grossed millions and millions of dollars in America alone—Beatle wigs, Beatle hats, Beatle Tee-shirts, Beatle eggcups, Beatlenut ice cream—
RINGO: Anytime you spell Beatle with an "a" in it, we get some money.

Q: How do you add up success?
ALL: Money.

Q: Mr. Starr is known for his rings. Mr. McCartney, obviously for his books* and Mr. Lennon for his wife. What about you Mr. Harrison? *(Ed. note: *Obviously this reporter had his Beatles crossed.)*
GEORGE: As long as I get an equal share of the money I'm willing to remain anonymous.

Q: What will you do when Beatlemania subsides?
JOHN: Count the money.

(Royal Command Variety Show with Princess Margaret and the Queen Mother in attendance.)
JOHN: The people in the cheap seats clap. The rest of you can rattle your jewelry.

Brian Epstein: That was quite a nice aircraft we flew back on.
RINGO: Let's buy it.

strawberry fields forever

'The Beatles are my secret weapon. If any country is in deficit to us—owes us money—I have only to say the Beatles are coming."

—Sir Alec Douglas-Home

'Sir Alec is trying to steal the Beatles from my Liverpool area constituency."

—Harold Wilson

"Queen Elizabeth has included the Beatles in birthday honors list, naming them members of the Most Excellent Order of the British Empire. They are the first group of pop singers to make the honors list. Henceforth, they may use the initials M.B.E. after their name."

—From the London newspapers,
June 11, 1965

Q: What was your reaction when you heard the news?
RINGO: There's a proper medal as well as the letters, isn't there? I will keep it to wear when I'm old. It's the sort of thing you want to keep.
JOHN: I thought you had to drive tanks and win wars to win the M.B.E.
GEORGE: I didn't think you got this sort of thing for playing rock 'n roll music.
PAUL: I think it's marvelous. What does this make my dad?

Hector Dupuis, a member of the Canadian House of Commons representing a Montreal district, has announced he is returning his M.B.E. medal because the Queen has awarded one to the Beatles. He claimed English royalty has placed him on the 'same level as vulgar nincompoops.' Mr. Dupuis received his medal for his work as director of selective service in Quebec."

From the Montreal newspapers,
June 14, 1965

Q: What do you say about Dupuis turning in his medal?
GEORGE: If Dupuis doesn't want the medal, he had better give it to us. Then we can give it to our manager, Brian Epstein. M.B.E. really stands for "Mr. Brian Epstein."

Q: Why do you think you got the medals?
JOHN: I reckon we got it for exports, and the citation should have said that. Look, if someone had got an award for exporting millions of dollars worth of fertilizer or machine tools, everyone would have applauded. So why should they knock us?

THE GREAT THRONE ROOM,
BUCKINGHAM PALACE
OCT. 26, 1965

The Beatles enter the great gilded room. Standing on a dais, dressed in a gold gown, is the Queen. She looks at the four boys and breaks into a big smile. George is wearing a blue suit, blue shirt and black tie. John, Paul and Ringo wear black suits with white shirts. At a signal from an usher they bow their heads and take four paces forward, halt before the Queen and bow again.

LORD COBBOLD (the Lord Chamberlain): John Lennon. George Harrison. Paul McCartney. Richard Starkey.

THE QUEEN: (to Paul) How long have you been together now?
PAUL: Oh, for many years.
RINGO: Forty years.
THE QUEEN: (to Ringo) Are you the one who started it?
RINGO: No, I was the last to join. I'm the little fellow.
THE QUEEN: (to John) Have you been working hard lately?
JOHN: No, we've been on a holiday.

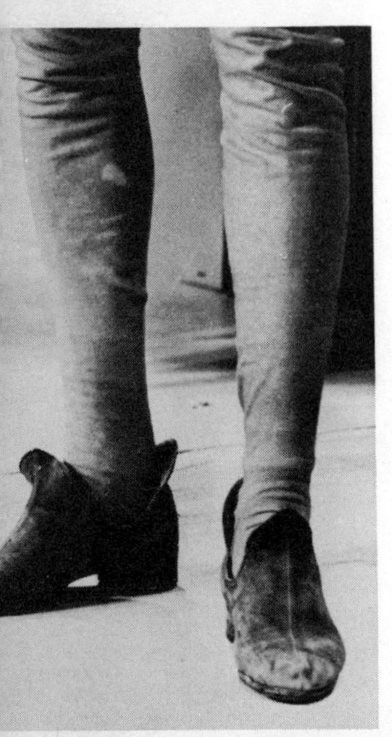

OUTSIDE THE WALLS OF
BUCKINGHAM PALACE

For the first time within memory a mob tries to invade the home of the Royal Family. Four thousand screaming teenagers struggle with police, shouting: "Long live the Queen! Long live the Beatles!

THE COURTYARD
BUCKINGHAM PALACE

PAUL: We've played many palaces including Frisco's Cow Palace. But never this one before. It's a keen pad and I liked the staff. Thought they'd be dukes and things but they were just fellahs.

Q: What about the Queen?
PAUL: She's lovely, great. She was very friendly. She was just like a mum to us.

Q: Were you nervous?
JOHN: Not as much as some of the other people in there.

Q: How did the other medal recipients act toward your award?
JOHN: One formally-dressed, middle-aged winner walked up to us after the ceremony and said: "I want your autographs for my daughter but I don't know what she sees in you." So we gave him our autographs.

Q: How did you know what to do during the ceremony?
JOHN: This big fellow *(an official from the Lord Chamberlain's office)* **drilled us. Every time he got to Ringo he kept cracking up.**

Q: What will you do with your medals?
PAUL: What you normally do with medals. Put them in a box.

PARKING RATES
I LOVE GEORGE
POLICE LINE
DO NOT CROSS
POLICE LINE

i want to hold your hand

In a London Club, British Labor Party leader Harold Wilson presents the "Show Biz" award to the Beatles and the ceremony breaks into bedlam. Millionaires jostle dukes for autographs of the Beatles.

* * *

As the Beatles go into their fifth number of the night at City Park Stadium in New Orleans, seven hundred screaming, bawling, clawing, crying, laughing teenagers come charging out of the stands toward the bandstand near the 10-yard line. They break through a police barrier and at the high water mark of their charge are about twenty feet from the Beatles—who sing on. Police leap over the barricades surrounding the stage, linking arms in an attempt to stop the teenage charge. The attempt fails and the police are forced to counter with their own charge. Floodlights go on, the Beatles sing on and the battle in front of the stage reaches epic proportions. Officers on crash trucks administer smelling salts to one hundred and fifty fainting females. Just as it looks as if the Beatles are going to be overrun, the ropes are brought out and behind them the police line holds firm. Mounted patrolmen assist in corralling the main element. Elsewhere on the horseshoe-shaped football field police are still tackling late comers to the riot. When order is restored, five teenagers are arrested. Two casualties, a boy with a broken jaw and a girl with a broken arm, refuse to leave the stadium until the concert is over. The performance ends with Paul shouting into the microphone; "**We want to thank everybody, including the football players.**"

EATLE WORSHIP
S IDOLATRY.
HE BIBLE
AYS, "CHILDREN
EEP YOURSELF
ROM IDOLS."
JESUS CHRIST,
PRAYER, THE
HOLY BIBLE,
AND PATRIOTISM
OUR NATIONS
ONLY HOPE...

"In the only popularity poll in Jesus' time, he came out second best to Barabbas..."
—The Rt. Rev. Kenneth Maguire, Angelican Bishop of Montreal

within you without you

"Experience has sown few seeds of doubt in him [John Lennon]; not that his mind is closed, but it's closed round whatever he believes at the time. 'Christianity will go,' he said. 'It will vanish and shrink. I needn't argue about that; I'm right and I will be proved right. We're more popular than Jesus now; I don't know which will go first—rock 'n roll or Christianity. Jesus was all right but his disciples were thick and ordinary. It's them twisting it that ruins it for me.'"

—From an interview with John Lennon by Maureen Cleave in the *London Evening Standard* March 4, 1966.

"John Lennon's remarks were taken out of context and did not accurately reflect the article or the subject as it was discussed. What actually occurred was a lengthy conversation between me and John in which the subject of Christianity was discussed. He observed that the power of Christianity was on the decline in the modern world and that things had reached such a ridiculous state that human beings—such as the Beatles—could be worshipped more religiously by people than their own religion. He did not mean to boast about the Beatles' fame."

—From a trans-atlantic radio interview with Maureen Cleave

JOHN: I'm not anti-God, anti-Christ or anti-religion. I was not saying we are greater or better.

"Mike Mitchell, program director of Longview radio station KLUE said here Wednesday that the station will join other stations in banning the playing of Beatle records as a result of the published comments by one of the singers on Jesus Christ...'We are...inviting local tennagers to bring in their records and other symbols of the group's popularity to be burned at a public bonfire on Friday night, August 13,' said Mitchell."

—*Longview* (Tex.) *Daily News*
Aug. 3, 1966

JOHN: I believe in God, but not as one thing, not as an old man in the sky. I believe that what people call God is something in all of us. I believe that what Jesus and Mohammed and Buddha and all the rest said was right. It's just that the translations have gone wrong.

"Deport the Beatles. They are unworthy of a decent American reception. They should be fumigated...They are undesirables and enemy agents to the Christian cause...They have been a corrupting influence...Parents in our country have no time for their lousy, low and lewd forms of so-called entertainment...Let them go back to Britain. As far as we're concerned, their concept of entertainment sounds as though it was conceived in sin and brought forth in iniquity—and some of the results it produces in youngsters tends to confirm our views."

—Carl L. Estes, Publisher of the
Longview (Tex.) *Daily News,* Aug. 12, 1966

Scene: South Carolina. The Grand Dragon of the State's Ku Klux Klan ties a Beatle record to a large wooden cross then sets the cross on fire.

Q: Are you sorry about your statement concerning Christ?
JOHN: I wasn't saying whatever they're saying I was saying. ...I'm sorry I said it, really. I never meant it to be a lousy anti-religious thing. From what I've read, or observed. Christianity just seems to me to be shrinking, to be losing contact.

JOHN: I wasn't saying the Beatles are better than God or Jesus. I used *Beatles* because it's easy for me to talk about Beatles. I could have said TV or the cinema or anything popular and I would have gotten away with it.

"I will revoke the membership of any member of my church who agrees with John Lennon's remarks about Jesus or who goes to see the Beatles."

—Rev. Thurman H. Babbs, pastor of the
New Heaven Baptist Church Cleveland, Ohio

JOHN: My views on Christianity are directly influenced by a book, *The Passover Plot,* by Hugh J. Schonfield. The premise in it is that Jesus' message had been garbled by his disciples and twisted for a variety of self-serving reasons by those who followed, to the point where it has lost validity for many in the modern age...The passage which caused all the trouble was part of a long profile Maureen Cleave was doing for the *London Evening Standard*...Then, the mere fact that it was in *Datebook* changed its meaning that much more.

Q: What was your own formal religious background?
JOHN: Normal Church of England, Sunday School and Sunday Church. But there was actually nothing going on in the church I went to. Nothing really touched us.

Q: How about when you got older?
JOHN: By the time I was 19, I was cynical about religion and never even considered about the goings on in Christianity. It's only in the last two years I—all the Beatles—have started looking for something else. We live in a moving hothouse. We've been mushroom-grown, forced to grow up a bit quick, like having 30-to-40-year-old heads in 20-year-old bodies.

We had to develop more sides, more attitudes. If you're a bus man, you usually have a bus man's attitude. But we had to sort of be more than four mopheads up on a stage. We had to grow up or we'd have been swamped.

Q: Why did you subject yourself to a public apology in front of television cameras?
JOHN: If I were at the stage I was five years ago, I would have shouted we'd never tour again and packed myself off and that would be the end of it. Lord knows I don't need the money. But the record burning. That was a real shock, the physical burning. I couldn't go away knowing that I created another little place of hate in the world. Especially with something as uncomplicated as people listening to records and dancing and playing and enjoying what the Beatles are. Not when I could do something about it. If I say tomorrow I'm not going to play again, I still couldn't live in a place with somebody hating me for something irrational.

Q: Why don't you tell your fans all this?
JOHN: But that's the trouble with being truthful. You try to apply truth talk, although you have to be false sometimes because the whole thing is false in a way, like a game. But you hope sometime that if you're truthful with somebody, they'll stop all the plastic reaction and be truthful back and it'll be worth it. But everybody is playing the game and sometimes I'm left naked and truthful with everybody biting me. It's disappointing.

From interview with Leroy F. Aarons:
Washington Post

"Beatle-burning teenagers, joined by a surprising number of adults, turned a huge pile of Beatle lore, records and pictures into a pile of ashes near the Radio Station KLUE tower Friday night. Tony Bridge, station owner, joined the campaign along with his staff members. Lowell Wolfe, station manager, aided Donna Woods, of Longview, at the bonfire, spreading kerosene on the pile."

—The *Longview* (Tex.) *Morning Journal*
Aug. 14, 1966.

"Radio Station KLUE was knocked off the air Saturday when a bolt of lightening struck the tall transmission tower. Lowell Wolfe, station manager, said Phil Ransom, news director, was knocked unconscious when the lightening coursed into the building...The lightening caused extensive damage to radio equipment but it was hoped the station would resume regular broadcasts today."

The *Longview* (Tex.) *Morning Journal,*
Aug. 14, 1966

lovely rita meter maid

Q: Would you ever accept a girl in your group if she could sing, play an instrument and wear the Beatle haircut?

RINGO: How tall is she?

she said she said

"The Beatles are nice young men, no doubt, but their music is horrible. They play electric guitars. Electric guitars are an abomination. Who ever heard of an electric violin? An electric cello? Or for that matter, an electric singer?"

—Andres Segovia

Q: (to George's mother vacationing in Rome) Are the Beatles going to play and sing for Pope Paul VI?

MRS. HARRISON: We heard the Beatles were asked to take part in the Cathedral dedication in Liverpool. And that the Pope may be there. If they perform before the Pope they will probably write something more suitable for the average church-goer.

POST NO BILLS
BEATLES

she loves you, yeah, yeah, yeah

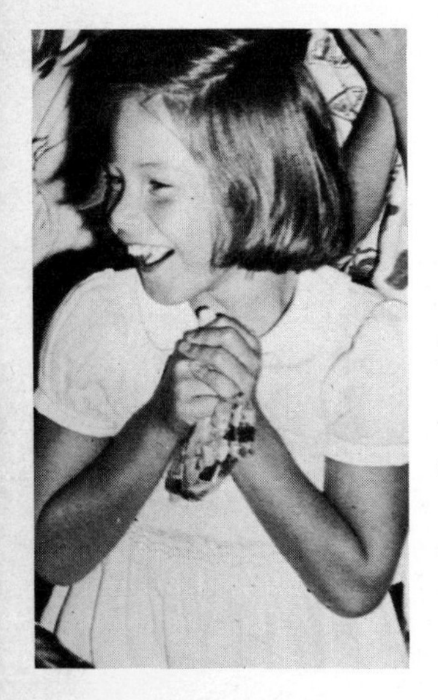

"I want to meet the Beatles because they have a special magic. When they perform the oppressing world crisis and other problems can be temporarily forgotten. They sing happy, swinging songs. I'd like to meet the four young men who can make everything seem a little brighter."

—Elaine May, 15, winner the *Indianapolis* (Ind.) News'"I Want to Meet the Beatles Because..."contest

*At the Edgewater Inn, a pier-side establishment in Seattle, Washington, a pretty teenage girl slips through Coast Guard boats and harbor police patrol by swimming fully clothed to underneath the Beatles' windows. She is fished out of the water by police before she can scale the wall.

*In Atlantic City, N. J., two thousand teenagers, mostly girls, surround the Beatles' motel quarters. In an alley on one side of the motel, two girls climb to a roof forty feet above the ground. They lower a long rope to ten other girls who scale the building. All twelve disappear into the motel before police can reach them.

*In Milwaukee's Coach House Inn, a mob of screaming teenagers storm the Beatles' recently vacated suite. They snatch up leftover eggs, toast, crackers and ash trays before police can throw them out.

*In New York City, two teenage girls perch precariously on the ledge of the Americana Hotel in hopes of seeing Paul. Paul, awakened from a nap in his suite at the Warwick Hotel, a block away, is on the way over to the Americana when two policemen grab the girls and pull them to safety.

*In Tokyo, Japanese girls charge the stage of a movie theatre during the showing of "A Hard Day's Night" to hug the screen.

"The Beatles display a few mannerisms which almost seem a shade on the feminine side, such as the tossing of their long manes of hair... Girls in very early adolescence still in truth find 'soft' or 'girlish' characteristics more attractive than rigidly masculine ones...They are still a little frightened of the idea of sex; therefore, they feel safer worshipping idols who don't seem too masculine."

—Dr. Joyce Brothers

you won't see me

JOHN: No more unscheduled public appearances. We've had enough. We're going to stay in our hotel except for concerts.
Q: Won't this make you feel like caged animals?
JOHN: No. We feed ourselves.

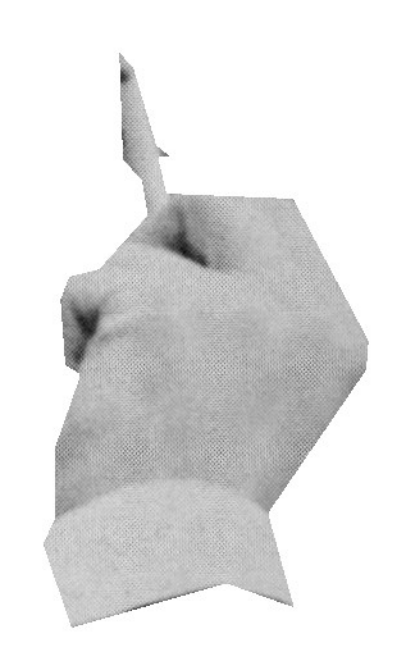

Q: Are you ever in any danger during your concerts?
PAUL: I was got once by a cigarette lighter. Clouted me right in the eye and closed my eye for the stay. In Chicago, a purple and yellow stuffed animal, a red rubber ball and a jump rope were plopped up on the stage. Had to kick a carton of Winston cigarettes out of the way when I played. And I saw a cigarette lighter go flying past me in Detroit's Olympia Stadium.

Q: Don't you worry about all that?
PAUL: It's o.k. as long as they throw the light stuff. Like paper.

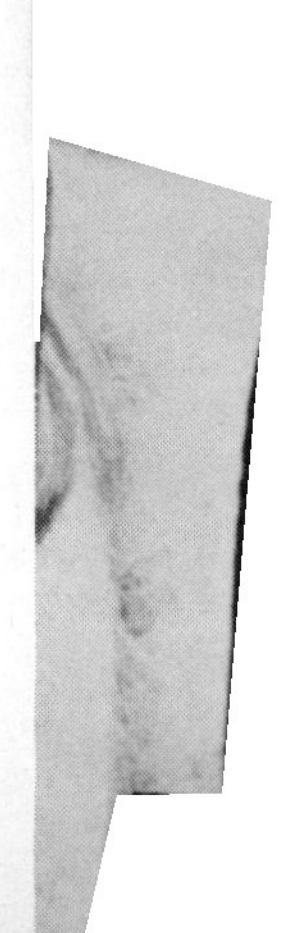

i've just seen a face

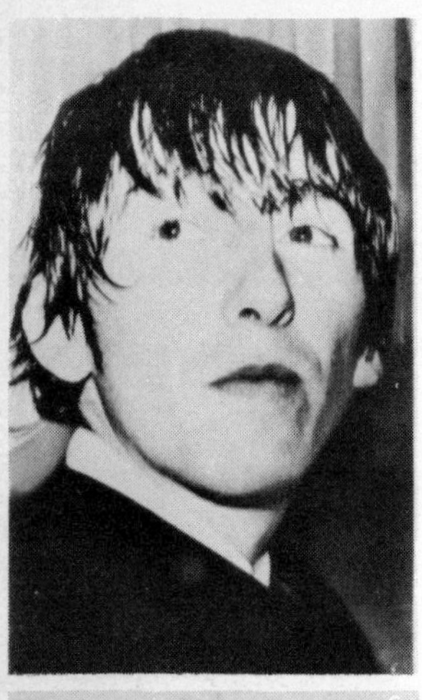

Q: Are you going to get haircuts over in America?
RINGO: What do you mean? We got them yesterday.

Q: Does your hair require any special attention?
JOHN: Inattention is the main thing.

Q: (from a woman reporter) Are you wearing wigs or real hair?
RINGO: Hey, where's the police?
PAUL: Take her out!
GEORGE: Our hair's real. What about yours, lady?

Q: What would happen if you all switched to crew cuts?
JOHN: It would probably be the end of the act.

Q: Do you ever think of getting a haircut?
GEORGE: No, luv. Do you?

Q: How do you feel about teenagers imitating you with Beatle wigs?
JOHN: They're not imitating us because we don't wear Beatle wigs.

Q: Where did you get your hair style?
PAUL: From Napoleon. And Julius Caesar, too. We cut it anytime we feel like it.
RINGO: We may do it now.

Q: What do you look like with your hair back on your foreheads?

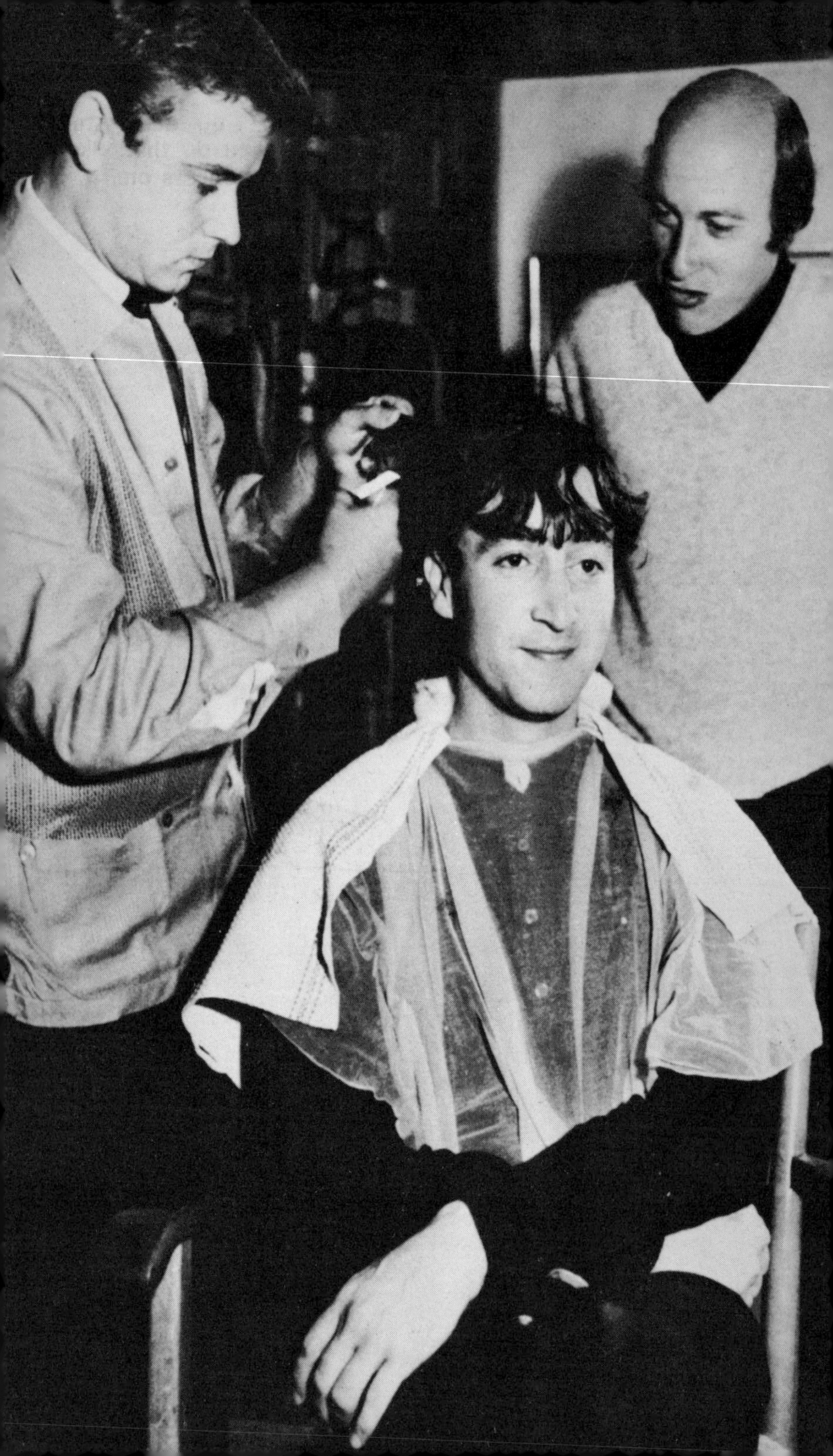

"I order the police: If there is a youth in Beatle hair, it must be cut!"

—Sukarno

JOHN: You just don't do that, mate. You feel naked if you do that, like you don't have any trousers on.

Q: Don't you feel icky and dirty with your hair so long, flopping in your eyes and down your neck?
JOHN: Of course not. We've got combs, you know.

Q: Where did you think up the hair-dos?
PAUL: We got them from a German photographer who wore his hair this way.
GEORGE: It was while we were in Germany. I went in swimming and when I came out, I didn't have a comb. So my hair just dried. The others liked it the way it looked and there we were.
JOHN: We've told so many lies about it we've forgotten.

run for your life

(Convention Hall, Atlantic City) Three hundred people are crowded into a press room for a Beatle interview. Nine are reporters. A man tries to present the Beatles with honorary U.S. citizenship papers. A little girl tries to hand them an oil portrait she did of them. The press conference turns into a massive contingent of screaming fans. Helmeted police wade through the mob with night sticks.

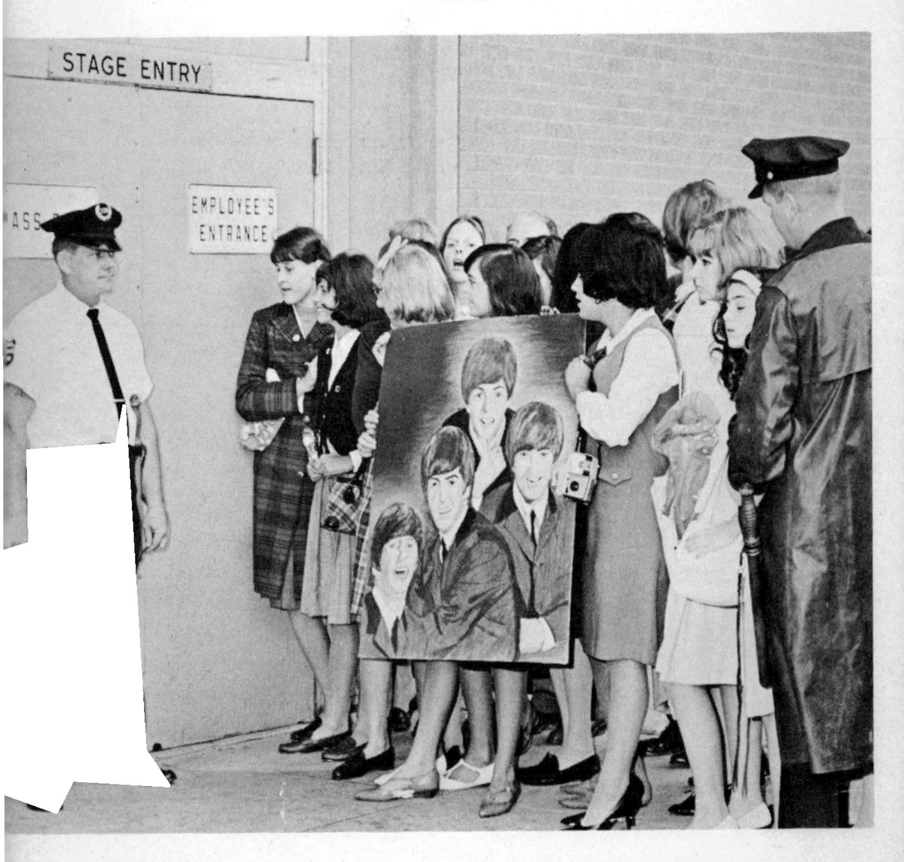

i want to tell you

PAUL: Someone in Los Angeles asked if Joan Baez would sing with us and Ringo said: "She sings at the drop of a bomb!"

PAUL: We kind of like the screaming teenagers. If they want to pay their money and sit out there and shout, that's their business. We aren't going to be like little dictators and say, "You've got to shut up." The commotion doesn't bother us anymore. It's come to be like working in a bell factory. You don't hear the bells after a while.

PAUL: Nothing annoys us really. Some things make us laugh. Like those "Stamp out the Beatles" gags. And the other day a photographer asked if he could take two pictures of us. One with our wigs on and one with our wigs off.

if i fell

Q: What did you think when your airliner's engine began smoking as you landed today?
RINGO: Beatles, women and children first!

"Only Hitler ever duplicated their power over crowds... I'm convinced they could sway a presidential election if they wanted to."
—Sid Bernstein, impresario for Beatles' N.Y. concerts

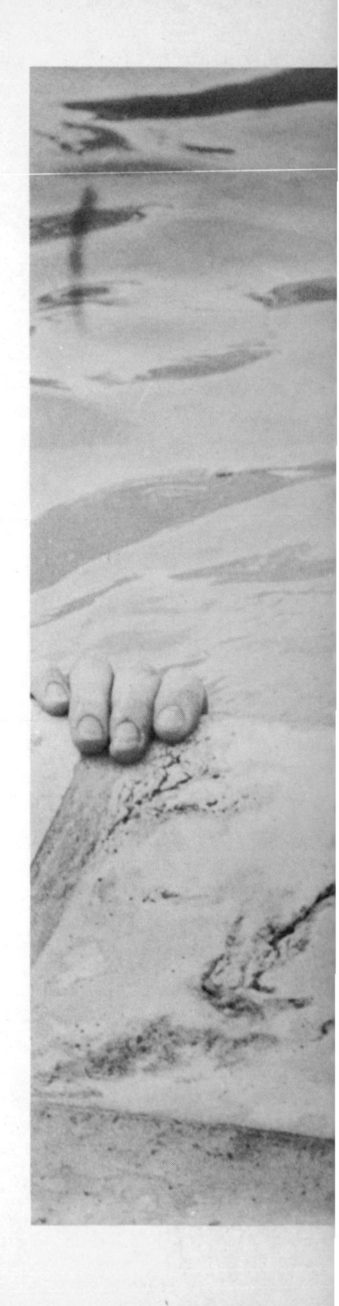

yellow submarine

Q: What about the lyrics to "YELLOW SUBMARINE"? Is there an allusion to narcotics?
RINGO: Nothing at all. It's simply a children's song with no hidden meanings. Many people have interpreted it to be a war song, that eventually all the world would be living in yellow submarines. That's not the case.

lucy in the sky with diamonds

Q: What are your feelings about LSD?
PAUL: I don't recommend it. It can open a few doors, but it's not any answer. You get the answers yourself.

"Lest anyone suggest my story today was excessively unsympathetic to the whole Beatle extravaganza...I left out the part about the Beatles' manager trying to get bellboys to lay hold of some illegal (2 o' clock in the morning) liquor for the lads...and I left out the information from one of the police guards about a 17-year-old fan in the lobby who allegedly was offering to copulate with anyone who would help her get up to the Beatles' penthouse suite..."

—From an office report turned in by a reporter for the Kansas City *(Mo.)* Star

run for your life

(Hanscom Field, Bedford, Mass.) One hundred and ten military policement flush out the weeds around the field for hiding teenagers. Thirty six state patrolmen prowl the runway perimeter. Police from Maynard, Concord, Lincoln and Bedford check every nook and cranny of nearby buildings for hiding teenagers. Only a small group of newsmen have been promised a peek at the Beatles. Their plane touches down and twenty state troopers spring like cats to block out newsmen a hundred yards away. Cars come whipping out from behind a building and the Beatles are rushed off the plane into them. Chaperoned by twenty-seven policemen, they arrive at the Hotel Madison in Boston where they are hurried into a side alley, hurled upon a freight elevator and safely whooshed up to their 11th floor suite.

a day in the life of . . . ringo

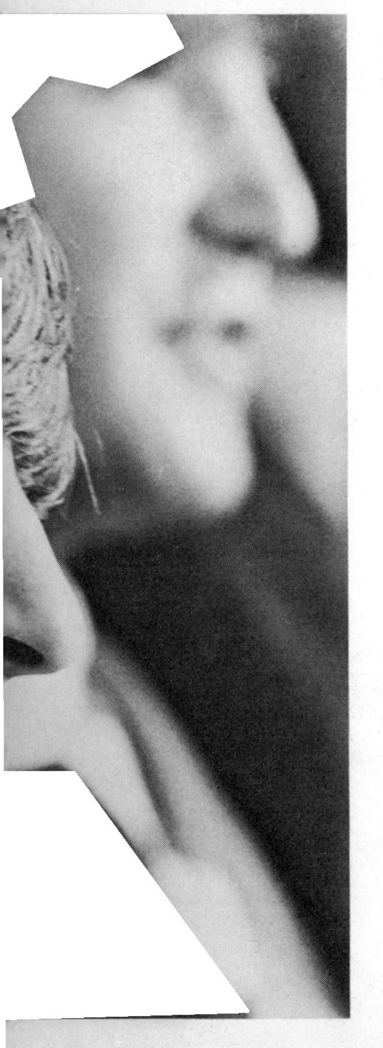

Scene: Exterior Speedway Motel, Indianapolis, Indiana
Time: 7 a.m., September 4, 1964

(Ringo walks out of the motel and heads toward three state patrolmen.)

RINGO: Can't sleep, chums. Suppose we go for a bit of a ride in the country. I'd like to see some of the sights around Indianapolis.
TROOPER: Sure! Hop in.

TROOPER: Say, would you mind coming to my house? I'd like my 11-year-old daughter to meet you.
RINGO: Sure.

Scene: Bedroom of farm house 25 miles north of Indianapolis

Trooper's daughter wakes up to find her father, two other state troopers and Ringo in her bedroom. She can hardly believe that she's not dreaming. Ringo talks to her and gives her his autograph. He is then invited to stay for breakfast, and he accepts.

He later joins the troopers for coffee.

Scene: A restaurant on U.S. 31

(Troopers and Ringo are drinking coffee. A woman walks up to Ringo.)

WOMAN: Can I have your autograph?
RINGO: Can you wait until I finish my coffee?
WOMAN: I'm in a hurry.
RINGO: Cheerio!

(Another woman walks up to Ringo.)

SECOND WOMAN: We—my family and I—drove all the way down from Kalamazoo, Michigan today, hoping to get a glimpse of the Beatles, but until now we were pretty unsuccessful.

(Ringo signs autographs for the whole family. A few minutes later a man walks up to Ringo's table, looks him over, then goes back to sit with his wife.)

MAN: (To wife) Did you see that jerk with the Beatle wig on?

Ringo has married Maureen Cox and the two hold an unscheduled press conference the next day at their "secret" hideaway. Surrounded by reporters and press photographers in the garden of a friend's house while teenage fans howl outside the wall, Ringo puts his arm around his new bride and says: "Alone at last, darling."

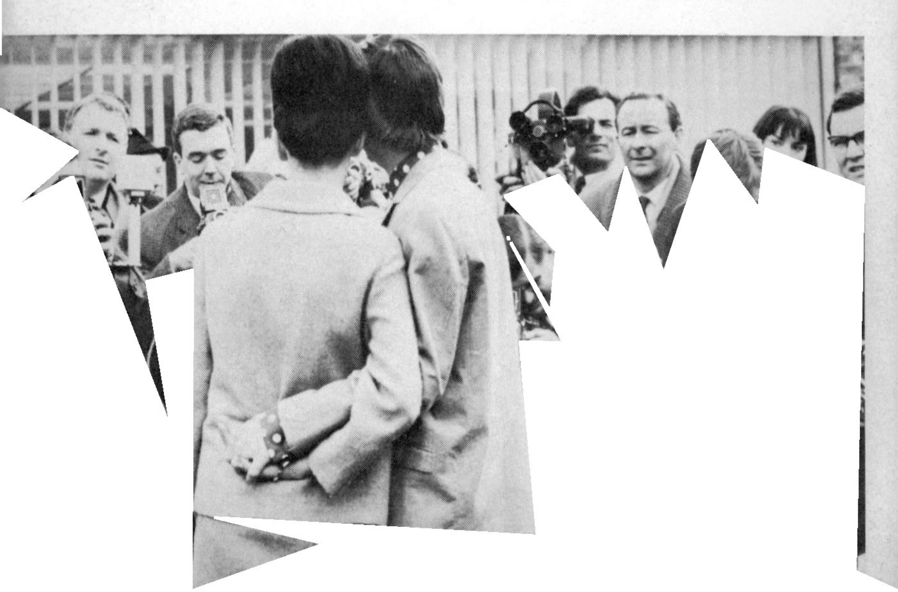

please please me

Q: What are your favorite programs on American television?

PAUL: "News in Español" from Miami. Popeye. Bullwinkle. All the cultural stuff.

JOHN: I like American TV because you can get eighteen stations, but you can't get a good picture on any one of them.

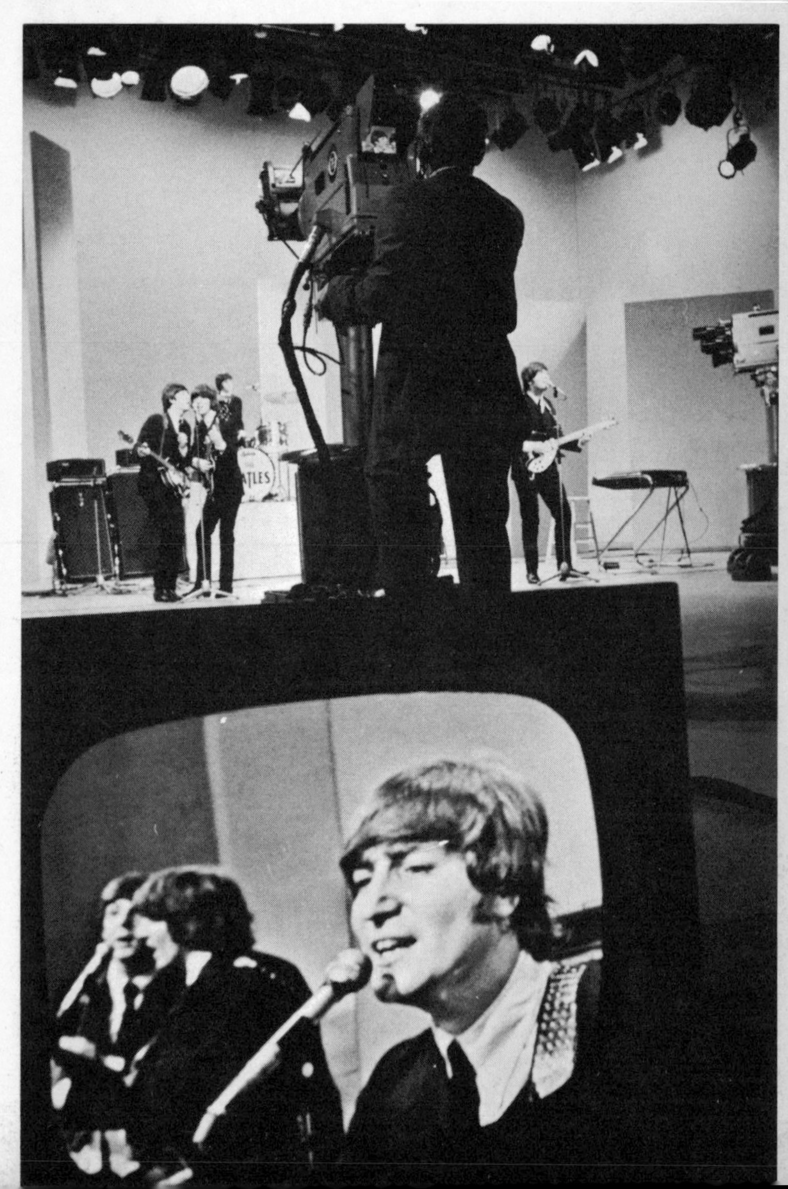

h r , th r and v rywh r

Q: You were at the Playboy Club last night. What did you think of it?
PAUL: The Playboy and I are just good friends.

Q: George, is the place you were brought up in a bit like Greenwich Village?
GEORGE: No. More like the Bowery.

Q: Ringo, how do you manage to find all those parties?
RINGO: I don't know. I just end up at them.
PAUL: On tour we don't go out much. Ringo's always out, though.
JOHN: Ringo freelances.

run for your life

(Seattle Center Coliseum) The Beatles have been trapped in their dressing room by screaming fans for almost an hour. Finally, a Red Cross ambulance is backed into the alley. A group of sailors climb in and the Beatles crawl in among them. Safely inside the darkened, locked ambulance, the Beatles escape undetected through the mob.

"Psycho-politicians are using the Beatle music and other innocuous sounding rythms to hypnotize American youth and prepare them for future submission to subversive control...a part of a systematic plan geared to making a generation of American youth mentally ill and emotionally unstable."

—From *Communism, Hypnotism and the Beatles* by David A. Noebel

paperback writer

PRINCE PHILLIP: (Presenting award for "the Most Outstanding Beat Group of the Year" and "Most Outstanding Vocal Group of the Year" to the Beatles.)
Which one of you wrote the book?
JOHN: (Raises his hand.) **Me, sir.**
PRINCE PHILLIP: I'll swap you one of mine for one of yours.
JOHN: Sure!
PRINCE PHILLIP: You don't know what you are letting yourself in for.

Q: John, what were you really trying to say in your book? Why don't people understand it?
JOHN: I understand it. If I wrote it in normal spelling there would be no point in writing. I'm not saying anything. There's no message.

Q: Why do you kill people off in your books?
JOHN: That's a good way to end them.

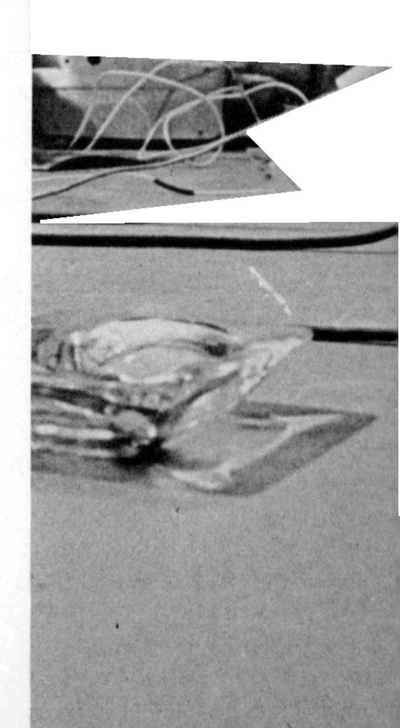

Q: How do you feel about bandleader Ray Block's statement that the Beatles won't last a year?
JOHN: We'll probably last longer than Ray Block.

Q: How come the Beatles, rather than 200 other groups, clicked?
RINGO: Sometimes I try to figure that out, too.

Q: What is the biggest threat to your careers, the atom bomb or dandruff?
RINGO: The atom bomb. We've already got dandruff.

Q: Sorry to interrupt you while you are eating, but what do you think you will be doing in five year's time when all this is over?
JOHN: Still eating.

Q: What would you do if the fans got past the police lines?
GEORGE: We'd die laughing.

Q: How long will your popularity last?
JOHN: When you're going to go, you're going to go.

Q: What will you do when the bubble bursts?
GEORGE: Take up ice hockey.
PAUL: Play basketball.

Q: Aren't you tired of all the hocus-pocus? Wouldn't you rather sit on your fat wallets?
PAUL: When we get tired, we take fat vacations on our fat wallets.

tomorrow never knows

Q: Do you get much fan mail?
RINGO: We get 2,000 letters a day.
JOHN: We're going to answer every one of them.

Q: Can we look forward to any more Beatle movies?
JOHN: Well, there'll be many more. But I don't know whether you can look forward to them or not.

Q: Are you afraid military service might break up your careers?
JOHN: No. There's no draft in England now. We're going to let you do our fighting for us.

Q: Is your popularity beginning to taper off?
PAUL: I agree that our popularity has hit a peak. But I also agreed with a man who said the same thing last year. And we were both wrong.

"I tell you, my friends, it [Beatlemania] is like seasickness, which is not a cultivated hallucinatory weakness, but something that derives from a lamentable and organic imbalance. If our children can listen avariciously to the Beatles it must be because through our genes we have transmitted to them a tendency to some disorder of the kind. What was our sin? Was it our devotion to Frank Sinatra? How could that be? We who worshipped at the shrine of purity. What then, gods and goddesses, was our sin, the harvest of what we now are reaping? We may not know what it was, even as Oedipus did not know during all those years, the reasons why he was cursed."

—William F. Buckley, Jr.

michelle

Q: Do any of you speak French?
PAUL: *Non.*

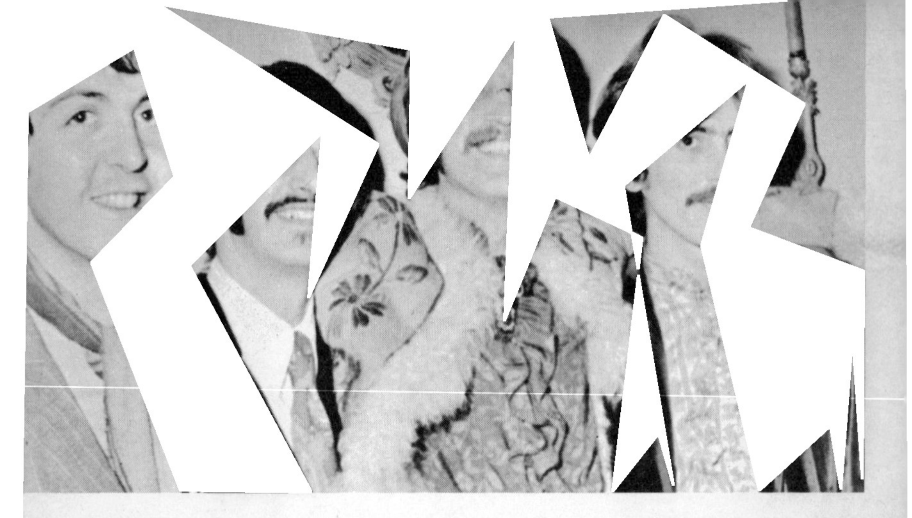

a little help from my friends

Q: What's the secret of your success?
JOHN: We have a press agent.
Q: Is it true none of you can read and write music?
PAUL: None of us can read or write music. The way we work it is like, we just whistle. John will whistle at me and I'll whistle back at him.

Q: Are you going to have a leading lady in the film you are about to make?
PAUL: We're trying to get the Queen. She sells in England, you know.

Q: Is it true that on one flight the stewardess broke up a pillow fight among you guys and got clobbered on the head?
GEORGE: I'm not really sure where she got hit. She did make us break it up though.

Q: Why don't all four of the Beatles ever sing together?
GEORGE: Well, we try to start out together, anyway.

REPORTER: Paul, you look like my son.
PAUL: You don't look a bit like my mother.

REPORTER: Why aren't you wearing a hat?
GEORGE: Why aren't you wearing a tie?

tell me why

Sample response of more than 1,500 entries in the *Washington Star's* "Ask the Beatles" contest:

"What happened to the irradiated calf's heart we sent you?"

"Does Paul really have six toes on his left foot?"

"What should I do for an avocado plant named 'Paul McCartney' with mildew on its leaves?"

"How many fillings do the Beatles have?"

"Do the Beatles like liver and spinach?"

"Is Paul related to a Venus Fly Trap because his mouth is always open?"

Q: Do teenagers scream at you because they are, in effect, revolting against their parents?
PAUL: They've been revolting for years.
JOHN: I've never noted them revolting.

run for your life

(Lafayette Motel, Atlantic City) The Beatles are smuggled out of their motel in the back of a fish delivery truck and ride undetected through the howling mob of teenagers.

the word

Q: Do you have any special messages for the Prime Minister and your parents?
JOHN: Hello, Alec.
GEORGE: Hello, Muddah.
RINGO: Hello, fellas.

Q: Do you have any special message for Dutch youth?
JOHN: Tell them to buy Beatle records.

Q: Do you have any advice for teenagers?
JOHN: Don't get pimples.

Q: How do you manage to have such a weird effect over teenagers?
GEORGE: Enthusiasm, I guess.

Q: Did you really use four letter words on the tourists in the Bahamas?
JOHN: What we actually said was "Gosh."
PAUL: We may have also said "Heavens!"
JOHN: Couldn't have said that, Paul. More than four letters.

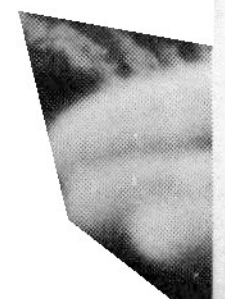

for no one

Q: Do you worry about smoking in public? Do you think it might set a bad example for your younger fans?
GEORGE: We don't set examples. We smoke because we've always smoked. Kids don't smoke because we do. They smoke because they want to. If we changed, we'd be putting on an act.
RINGO: (loud whisper) **We even drink.**

do you want to know a secret

Q: What careers would you individually have chosen had you not become entertainers?
RINGO: A hairdresser.
GEORGE: I had a short go at being an electrician's apprentice, but I kept blowing things up so I got dumped.
PAUL: I don't know...maybe something with art in it.
JOHN: No comment.

Q: Who in the world would the Beatles like to meet more than anyone else?
RINGO: The real Santa Claus.

Q: Which of you is really bald?
GEORGE: We're all bald. And I'm deaf and dumb.

Q: Do any of you have ulcers?
GEORGE: None that we've noticed.

Q: What is your favorite food?
RINGO: I'm hung up on hamburgers.
GEORGE: All four of us are mad about Hero sandwiches.
PAUL: I have a yen for grilled cheese sandwiches.
JOHN: George and I usually wait until someone else orders, then say, "I'll have that too."

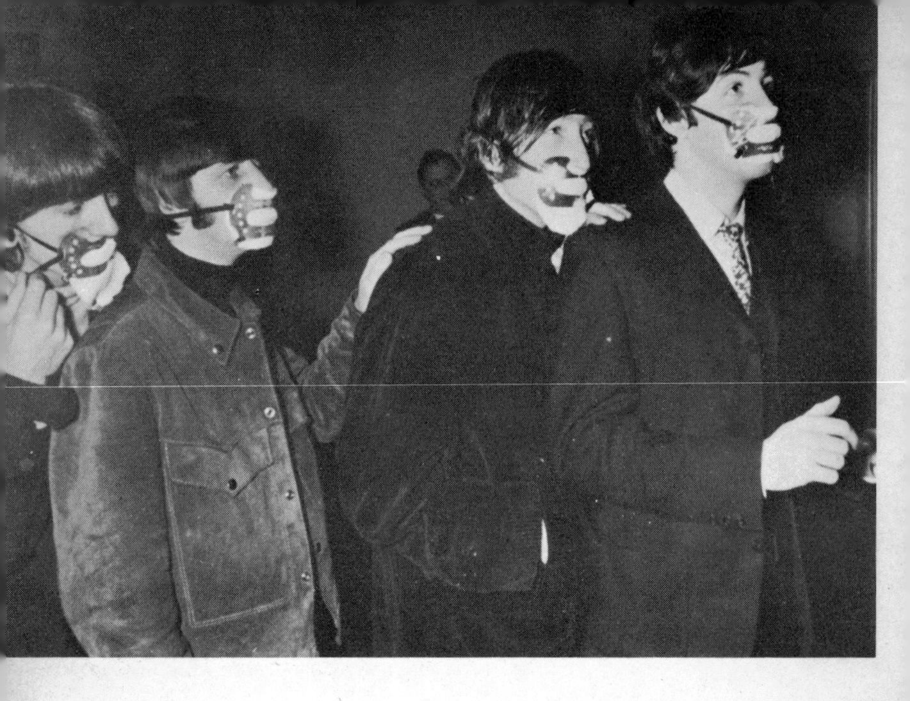

run for your life

(Seattle-Tacoma Airport) The plane carrying the Beatles to Vancouver, B.C. has turned back and landed again in Seattle. The Beatles forgot to have their passports stamped.

"The same trance-like state observed on the faces of Beatle fans were also portrayed on the faces of girls on Greek vases fashioned in 600 B.C. ...The human nervous system has not changed in a half-a-million years. Feelings of fear and anger are essential for conversion and brainwashing and can be accelerated by rhythmic preparation with drums and dancing. Hitler prepared his people for war with similar methods and twenty million people were killed.

—Dr. William Sargant, Chief of psychological medicine at St. Thomas' Hospital, London

i am the walrus

Q: How come you were turned back by immigration?
JOHN: We had to be deloused.

Q: How do you feel about the invasion of your privacy all the time?
RINGO: The only time it bothers us is when they get us to the floor and really mangle us.

Q: What does each Beatle consider his two most valued possessions?
JOHN: Our lives.

mr. taxman

The most conservative estimates put the net worth of George and Ringo at $3,000,000 each, and of John and Paul at $4,000,000—because of their extra earnings as song writers. The figures could be—and quite possibly are—twice as high.

Q: What do you do with your money?
RINGO: We bury it.
GEORGE: We hide it.
PAUL: We don't see it. It goes to our office.
JOHN: We pay a lot of taxes.

"I will exchange two tickets to the Beatles concert for a good car."
—Classified ad in a Hamburg, Germany newspaper

getting better

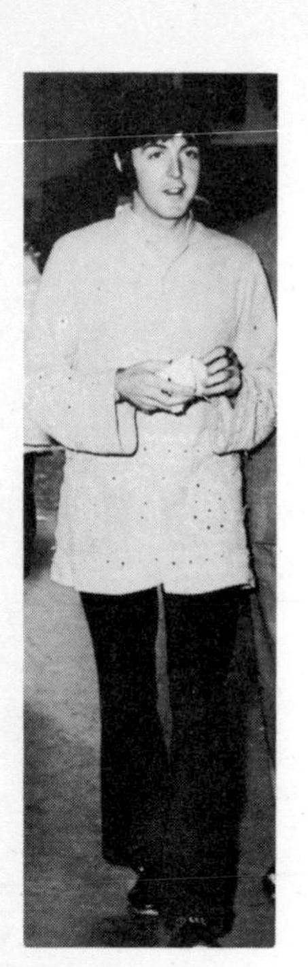

Q: What are your feelings on the "hints of queerness" American males found in the Beatles during the early days of your climb to popularity?
PAUL: There's more terror of that hint of queerness—of homosexuality—here than in England where long hair is more accepted. Our whole promotion made us look silly. But we've had a chance to talk to people since then and they can see we're not thick little kids.

Q: Has success spoiled the Beatles?
JOHN: Well, you don't see us running out and buying bowler hats, do you? I think we've pretty well succeeded in remaining ourselves.
PAUL: The great thing about it is that you don't have big worries anymore when you've got where we have—only little ones, like whether the plane is going to crash.

Q: What's it like being Beatles?
GEORGE: We've gotten to know each other quite well. We can stand each other better now than when we first met.

fixing a hole

RINGO: The four of us have had the most hectic lives. We have got almost anything money can buy. But when you can do that, the things you buy mean nothing after a time. You look for something else, for a new experience. It's like your Dad going to the boozer and you want to find out what the taste of drink is like. We have found something now which fills the gap. Since meeting His Holiness, Maharishi Mahesh Yogi, I feel great.

PAUL: I now realize that taking drugs was like taking an aspirin without having a headache.

JOHN: If we'd met Maharishi before we had taken LSD, we wouldn't have needed to take it.

GEORGE: We haven't really started yet. We've only just discovered what we can do as musicians, what thresholds we can cross. The future stretches out beyond our imagination.

hello goodbye

Q: What do you plan to do after this?
RINGO: What else is there to do?

PHOTO CREDITS

UNITED PRESS INTERNATIONAL: Cover photographs. Page 2, top; center. Page 3, top right, center right, bottom left. Page 12. Page 14. Page 18. Page 19, top. Page 24, bottom. Pages 28-29. Page 36. Page 40, top. Page 53. Page 56. Page 59. Page 65. Page 66. Page 67. Pages 68-69. Page 74, top, bottom. Page 75.
WIDE WORLD PHOTOS: Page 2, bottom right. Page 7, top center; right. Page 8. Page 9. Page 10, top. Page 13. Pages 16-17. Page 19, bottom. Pages 20-21. Page 22, top. Page 25. Pages 26-27. Page 32. Page 44. Page 45, top, bottom. Page 46. Page 47, bottom left, bottom right. Page 49. Page 58. Pages 62-63. Page 72. Pages 76-77. Page 78.
LARRY MULVEHILL: Page 2, left. Page 15. Page 39.
GEORGE HONEYCUTT, HOUSTON (TEX.) CHRONICLE: Page 2, bottom. Page 47, top.
POPSIE: Page 3, top left. Page 5.
KEN HEINEN, WASHINGTON (D.C.) STAR: Page 7, top left.
WILLIAM LA FORCE JR., BALTIMORE (MD.) SUN: Page 7, left center, bottom left. Pages 30-31, top. Page 41. Page 42. Page 48. Page 73.
GARY SETTLE, TOPEKA (KAN.) CAPITAL-JOURNAL: Pages 10-11, bottom. Page 24, top.
GALAXY INTERNATIONAL: Pages 22-23. Page 43. Pages 50-51. Page 52. Page 64. Page 70. Page 71.
TED ROZUMALSKI, BLACK STAR: Pages 30-31, bottom. Page 40, bottom. Pages 54-55. Pages 60-61.
OWEN DUVALL, WASHINGTON (D.C.) STAR: Page 38.
CHARLES ALLEN, LERNER HOME NEWSPAPERS, CHICAGO (ILL.): Page 57.

If you would like additional copies of this book for your friends, you may purchase them from your local bookseller or send $1.00 (each book desired) in check or money order – no currency or C.O.D.'s please – to:

Grosset & Dunlap, Inc.
51 Madison Avenue
New York, N.Y. 10010
Dept. JS

Please allow 3 weeks for delivery.